WINNERS AND LOSERS

HOW ELECTIONS WORK IN AMERICA